Peercoin

I0484169

The Ultimate Beginner's Guide for Understanding Peercoin and What You Need to Know

presentation of the information is without contract or any type of guarantee assurance.

The trademarks that are used are without any consent, and the publication of the trademark is without permission or backing by the trademark owner. All trademarks and brands within this book are for clarifying purposes only and are the owned by the owners themselves, not affiliated with this document.

Table Of Contents

Introduction

This book is for people who are interested in learning more about the Peercoin currency and are not sure where to start or what information to rely on. I made this book in response to the high demand of people wanting to know more about Peercoin and why there is so much hype around it.

The Internet today has many articles and misinformation about Peercoin that confuse people who are interested in learning about this revolutionary cryptocurrency and possibly interested in purchasing some Peercoins themselves.

In this book, I am going to give you a short, concise guide for everything you need to know to get started with Peercoin. The history of this currency as well as the current innovations that are going on in the Peercoin market are key to understanding what the future will hold. We will also go over the different functions and options that a person has when it comes to purchasing their own Peercoin and how to use them.

And most importantly, we will go through the pros and cons of using Peercoin so that you can understand everything you need to know before taking the plunge and investing in it yourself. Whether you plan on diversifying from Bitcoin, buying your first cryptocurrency in Peercoin, or you just want to know more about why this trend is becoming so popular, it is important to know all the benefits and risks involved. This book also highlights Peercoin's differences from other similar cryptocurrencies.

Cryptocurrency became popular in 2009 in the form of Bitcoin. Bitcoin was designed and developed to use a hybrid system of proof-of-stake and proof-of-work to address different vulnerabilities, such as mining monopoly and inflation. As cryptocurrency is being introduced to decentralize the production of money, Peercoin is becoming one of the most prominent names in the cyptocurrency arena. Also called PPCoin, P2P, and peer-to-peer coin, Peercoin (unofficially coded PPC), already has one of the largest market capitals, with 100 million dollars, as of February 2014.

I recommend that you take notes while you are reading the book. This will ensure that you get the most out of the information in here. I want you to feel that you made a purchase that is worth your money and you can look over the notes of this book even after you've finished reading it. The notes will help you to pinpoint exactly what you need to implement and by writing things down, you will be able to recall specifics and how to handle certain situations when they arise.

Lastly, remember that everything in this book has been compiled through research, my own experiences, as well as the experiences of others, so feel free to question what you have read in this book. I encourage you to do your own research on the things that you want to look deeper into. The more you understand about Peercoin, the more educated your decision-making process will be when it comes to purchasing and transacting your own, or giving advice   to   others.

Chapter 1:

Cryptocurrency

The idea of cryptocurrency first occurred to David Chaum when he tried to incorporate cryptography with electronic money in developing DigiCash and eCash. He used cryptography, a method of using secret codes and ciphers, to make electronic money transactions anonymous.

This idea led to the birth of cryptocurrency. The same principle was introduced by Satoshi Nakamoto in 2009, when he/she developed Bitcoin (BTC), the first-ever digital cryptocurrency designed to decentralize the distribution of money using a proof-of-work scheme.

Cryptocurrencies are produced by a collective system that makes use of complex mathematical problems for mining. Unlike fiat money where the value of the money is determined by what the central bank declares, the value of a cryptocurrency is determined by its users and those who accept it for trading.

Bitcoin, the forerunner in the new generation of cryptocurrencies, started as a design of a new currency that makes use of cryptography and open-source software, so that it can be used to purchase goods and services. It was created as a currency that would be completely decentralized, away from the eyes of central banks and immune from government manipulations. Its developer decided that only 2 billion U.S. dollars' worth of Bitcoins would be produced, almost 6 million dollars of which have been mined in its first four years of existence.

Cryptocurrency vs. Traditional Currency

The main difference between traditional currency and cryptocurrency is that the former's value is dependent on what institutions have specified. The value of a cryptocoin can be specified by the person who is about to take it from its original owner. For example, a bitcoin's value can be discussed by people who will agree as to how much one coin is worth. If both agree that one bitcoin is worth $500.00, then that bitcoin will be worth $500.00, all throughout the system. A cryptocurrency's value is also based on its scarcity. Since coins are produced to reach only a certain number, exchanges for one coin can be very high.

Unlike a traditional fiat currency with stable and definite value, a cryptocurrency's value is volatile. Since the worth of the coin depends on how much the other party is willing to pay, the value of the coin can change on a daily basis. Because of this, business owners accepting cryptocurrency for payment are taking a big risk, as the value of what someone paid today can drop drastically the next day.

Traditional currencies needs a wallet, a vault, or a bank account to be kept safe. Cryptocurrencies only need your virtual wallet or a hard drive for safekeeping. Aside from that, unlike traditional currency, that is prone to forgery or counterfeiting, digital money is counterfeit-proof. Cryptocoin miners have a ledger that keeps a record of all coins produced (or in other words, hashed) all over the world.

For example, a cryptocoin has an encryption of 254-33456789-000-222. This encryption will be listed in the ledger used by the coin's server, together with the pseudonym of the person who mined it first, then who he traded it to, the third person to receive the coin through an exchange, and so on. This will make it extremely difficult for people to create counterfcits, thus, making it a secure means of payment.

The anonymity that comes with cryptocoins is also a distinguishing factor. Although these coins' codes are logged in a common ledger, the names that are listed down are pseudonyms. No true identity can be found in the ledger. It's impossible to really know who bought what and whose virtual wallet it will land in next. What most people don't like about this is the fact that if cryptocurrency becomes a widely accepted means of payment, the black market will get the chance to exercise free enterprise and authorities would have limited power to prohibit such exchanges.

Pros and Cons of Cryptocurrency

While digital money is now being used to pay for products and services, such as pizza and in-app or in-game purchases, and while prominent companies all over the internet already accept the said currency, there are still some discussions and issues regarding its use. Let's start with the good:

The confidentiality and anonymity of purchases can be very convenient.

This means that if you are the type of person who likes surprising your partner with things like a flower bouquet delivery or a weekend trip to Cabo, she's not likely to find out what you bought, who you bought it from, and/or whether you bought anything at all. Unlike when you use your credit or debit card, which would show all of your purchases on your monthly statement in your account, cryptocurrency ledgers only make use of the pseudonym of the owner of the coin.

It will not reveal anything about the agency or the person you bought your gifts from, as well as the description of what has been traded. Because of this, you are not likely to be found out before the time you're supposed to give that gift or go on   that   trip.

It is completely decentralized and its value is not affected by institutional manipulations and is fraud-free.

The authenticity of a cryptocoin is found in its code, and that's something one cannot easily counterfeit (remember the ledger discussed earlier and how codes can only be associated with one coin). Using Bitcoin's protocol as an example, cryptocurrency transactions are irreversible, making it ideal for merchants accepting online and POS payments.

Unlike in traditional currency where serial numbers can be counterfeited – real and fake ones are very hard to tell apart. Using cryptocurrencies isn't like using credit and debit cards either, where card identity theft poses a huge problem.

Very low fee, if not free, for payment transactions.

From a merchant's point of view, the seller shouldn't really shoulder bank surcharges for international money transfers and credit/debit card payments, so this means that the customers are going to be charged an additional fee to cover for these transaction costs. That's alright if you're running a big business and your target market is the elites.

What about the low-margin businesses that can't afford to lose customers just because of an extra charge? In cryptocurrency trading, the seller is allowed to set the transaction fee to be collected. Merchants can even set this transaction fee to zero (0.00) if they wish, making it less costly than banking and card payments.

Now for the negatives:

The volatile nature of its value is quite risky.

When a merchant accepts cryptocoins for payment, it presents itself as a risk of possible loss. Cryptocoin payment facilities are developed to accept payments to be converted later into the merchant's currency of choice. Let us say that "person A" buys something from "business B" using two peercoins, and the current exchange rate is US $150.00/PPC.

If the value of peercoin suddenly decreased to US $100.00/PPC before the seller had the chance to convert the coins to US fiat currency, he automatically loses US $50.00 for that transaction   alone.

Cryptocurrency can be a means to support the black market.

Yes, purchases being anonymous is great when we talk about confidentiality during transactions. Unfortunately, it also poses an opportunity for illegal transactions and/or sellers of illegal items. This means that pirated copies of every item in the world, unlicensed weapons, and even prohibited drugs could be sold to people without any detail of who those things went to and who sold them. In addition, since law enforcement agencies have no records whatsoever of the transactions that took place, it would be impossible for them to penalize people or file charges against them.

Since it is digital, it is prone to hacking and malware.

It sounds great to know that you do not have to worry about leaving your money at home when you are shopping, as long as you have your hard drive with you. Paying for things will be possible anytime and anywhere. However, just like any other digital or electronic gadget and sources, digital currency can be stolen or destroyed by "computer geniuses."

It is true that you may save your crypto-money in your virtual wallet or even on a cloud, but once hackers get access to these accounts, you may as well say goodbye to your hard-earned coins. We all know how flash drives, hard drives, and memory cards can be infected with viruses and malwares that can destroy your entire file/folder and consequently, your coins.

Cryptocurrency is a great innovation, especially in the field of commerce and finance. It does have its good and bad points, but it's still too soon to say that these negative sides cannot be fixed. In four years, right after Bitcoin was developed, numerous cryptocurrencies following the same protocol as that of Bitcoin have been introduced – some of them using similar functions, some integrating new schemes, and some are complete copy-cats, but all of them try to introduce an alternative to actual currencies and payment systems.

Chapter 2:

Peercoin Begins

Now that you know what cryptocurrency is and how it all began, it will be easier for you to understand Peercoin and its system.

Peercoin (code: PPC, PPCoin, P2P coin, peer-to-peer coin) was developed by Sunny King (pseudonym) and Scott Nadal in 2012. Eventually, Nadal ceased to contribute to the development of PPC, making Sunny King the currency's sole developer. Although inspired by Bitcoin, Peercoin is developed to address the issues of its forerunner. Presently, it is the only cryptocurrency to use a hybrid of proof-of-stake (PoS) and proof-of-work (PoW) schemes, making PPC even better than BTC.

The Peercoin System

Peercoin prides itself on being the first and only real peer-to-peer cryptocurrency to date. This is because, unlike other alternative coins, PPC allows its entire community to mine for coins and determine its price collectively. There are also many different things that set Peercoin apart from its counterparts.

Proof-of-work Scheme

Using the same SHA-256 used by Bitcoin, Peercoin was initially developed to perform the same way. In the PoW scheme, a computer system will be used to process an equation needed to generate hashes to create coins. As more coins are generated and as more people start mining, equations become harder to process and the difficulty of creating coins will increase over time.

Proof-of-stake Scheme

The proof-of-stake feature of Peercoin is developed to address the 51% attack problem that exists in Bitcoin. The proof-of-work system used by Bitcoin can make one user in charge of 51% of the coins being generated, which can later lead to monopoly. As one person gets the greater half of the whole system, he can be allowed to make use of the same coin twice.

Proof-of-stake will regularize this by making the generation of coins dependent on the actual holdings of an entity. For example, if an entity is currently holding 2% share for the entire system-generated peercoins, he is only entitled to 2% of the proof-of-stake coins. This will eliminate the possibility of double-spending coins and market monopoly.

Energy-Efficient Mining

One of the problems of cryptocoin mining is high energy consumption. This is also being addressed by Peercoin with its PoS scheme. As mentioned earlier, cryptocurrencies are generally produced using PoW, which makes use of high-powered cryptographic computer systems to create hashes that will be used for the coins' codes. What makes Peercoin stand out is how it is initially supposed to be hashed like that, but as the stakes increase and the mining becomes difficult, the incentive to mint (coin mining) decreases.

So, the main generation of coins will be mostly based on PoS – for which, only the client software will be needed. This means that the use of the high-powered computers will decrease, which will subsequently result in lower power or energy consumption.

Inflation and Deflation Aspects

As coins become harder to generate, Peercoin is viewed to have a steady inflation rate of 1% per annum. Combining the PoS and PoW schemes, allow peercoins to be generated at a rather slow pace. Although its market cap is around 2 billion, which is unlikely to be generated in a year's time, such a limit is set for checkpoint purposes only. This means that unlike Bitcoin, Peercoin can be used for a long time and the supply of the currency is limitless.

An amount of 0.01 PPC/transaction is being levied to the entity involved. This 0.01 PPC will not be given to the miner, but will be destroyed to solve issues of inflation. The developer and his team will solve the issue of inflation by collecting higher transaction fees as the currency's economic activity grows. This is to encourage entities to save more during deflation and spend more during inflation.

Store Rather than Transfer

Many will not understand, and possibly run away from, the 0.01 PPC minimum transaction fee for Peercoin. What you should keep in mind, however, is that if you look into the design of Peercoin, you will see how it aims to be the backbone of other cryptocurrencies. It does not wish to overrule the existence of other currencies, it wishes to be the support for these currencies whenever possible. The transaction fee for PPC will give it the needed support when inflation arises. This makes Peercoin more stable and less volatile, as compared to other cryptocurrencies.

Also, there's the idea that Peercoin is not meant to be used for small purchases, it is meant to be a stock of value. If you are to spend $100.00 for your online purchase and we will assume that you will need 10.50 PPC to complete the transaction, would you still go through with it? You probably wouldn't. It would be best to keep that 10.50 PPC in storage and convert it to traditional currency later, sort of like investing through a bank and reaping interest later.

Chapter 3:

Altcoins and Their Differences

Aside from Peercoin and Bitcoin, there are many other alternative (Altcoins) cryptocurrencies used in the market today. The list below shows the most commonly used on the internet, and gives a brief description of each.

Litecoin (LTC)

Charles Lee, a former Google employee, introduced Litecoin in 2011. It is an open-source software P2P currency that is almost identical to Bitcoin. The significant differentiating aspect of Litecoin from Bitcoin is the former's block generation, which is 2.5 minute/block as compared to Bitcoin's 10 minute/block. Litecoin also uses memory-hard script in its PoW algorithm function. Lastly, LTC seeks to produce four times more units than Bitcoin.

Dogecoin (DOGE)

Dogecoin is now being widely used as a tipping system for users who provide interesting and quality content on social media platforms. Unlike other cryptocurrencies, DOGE aims to circulate approximately 100 billion coins by the end of 2014, with the additional generation of 5.2 billion coins annually.

Billy Markus, DOGE's creator, initially created it to be a cryptocurrency that would reach a wider demographic segment than Bitcoin and eventually distance it from Bitcoin's controversial involvement in the Silk Road drug marketplace. Dogecoin became a great name in terms of charity donations and social works when it donated hundreds of dollars to athletes who could not afford to go to the 2014 Sochi Winter Olympics.

Namecoin (NMC)

Namecoin is a cryptocurrency that also acts as a decentralized DNS alternative. Its main function is to facilitate payment for domain name registrations that would avoid domain name censorship. Aside from domain name purposes, Namecoin is also proposed to be used for identity systems, personal namespaces, notary or timestamp systems, alias systems, etc.

Primecoin (XPM)

Also developed by Sunny King, Primecoin makes use of a scheme similar to that of Peercoin. It also features fast generation of coin blocks and fast confirmation of transactions. The block rewards one can get from mining are not fixed, rather, it is always 999 divided by the square of the mining difficulty. So, technically speaking, the block rewards you will get will be adjusted to the level of difficulty during mining.

Primecoins use prime number chains, which are the Cunningham chain (first kind), the Cunningham chain (second kind), and the Bi-twin chain.

Ripple (XRP)

Ripple, unlike other cryptocurrencies, is a payment system that allows users to pay for their purchases using a cryptographic signed system and denominated in real-world currencies and assets. These payments are recorded as debts, and the credit line of the involved entities are then adjusted after the transaction.

Ripple was developed by Ripple Labs to be a bridge currency for any fiat money, cryptocurrency, and other values such as air miles, mobile minutes, and the likes.

Chapter 4:

Your First Peercoin Wallet

Your Peercoin success will start by setting up your peer-coin wallet. The Peercoin wallet will be your virtual wallet, or bank account, that will store your peercoins.

The first step is to install your wallet:

You may visit Peercoin's site at www.peercoin.net and from there, you will see a big button that says "Download Wallet."

Choose your computer's operating system from the list of links provided on their website. Currently, Peercoin wallet is supported on Windows, Mac OS X, and Linux devices. Additional instructions are provided on the website, so that you don't have to worry about what steps to take.

If you will be using PPCoin-QT, you have to set up or configure your wallet and create a *ppcoin.conf* folder in your wallet directory. You will also need to change or add *server=1* to the *ppcoin.conf* folder that you created.

Lastly, change or set your password. The default password is *rpcpassword*. You will need to set it to something more secure. If you are using *ppcoind* and you fail to set your password, you will get a computer-generated one.

I strongly recommend visiting the site while setting up your PPC wallet, as the site has a sample configuration you can use as a basis. After setting up your wallet, you will now be ready to mine and exchange your coins.

Your peercoin wallet will have the following tabs:

Overview

It will give you an overview of how much you have in your wallet, your stakes, your transaction count, and your unconfirmed transactions.

Send Coins

This tab will let you send coins to any public address for payment or transfer.

Receive Coins

This tab is where you can see if someone would like to send coins to your address. You can also use this tab to scan your QR code in case you do not know your public address. It is fairly easy to paste your code somewhere else.

Transactions

This tab will show you all of your past and current transactions, whether sending coins or receiving coins.

Address Book

This tab contains addresses you have saved in your wallet.

Export

This tab is used to export your wallet settings to other folders or devices.

Peercoin Mining

Now that you have your wallet, you may start mining your peercoins. Peercoin is compatible with ASIC hardware, which is also used to mine on Bitcoin networks. There are also mining pools that allow all participants to mine together, finding coin blocks and sharing the rewards based on their Peercoin shares. A wallet owner can mine at:

https://peercoin.blockmines.com

https://peercoin.ecoining.com

https://ppcoin.d7.lt

http://ppc.fixx.ru

https://hynodeva.com

https://coinotron.com/coinotron/AccountServle
t?action=home

https://www.multipool.us

NOTE: Different mining tools use different rates of fees and payout systems. Study your mining pool carefully and consult the host for clarification before you register for a mine.

Peercoin Minting

Peercoin minting is the act of gaining "interest" for your Peercoin stake, as discussed earlier in the proof-of-stake portion of this book. In minting, you need to wait at least 30 days until your coins mature and gain interest before you can start the process. Just remember the following if you want to mint your Peercoin:

You get what you put at stake. This means that if you have a 1% stake, you will also get 1% mint of that total stake. To explain it further, let us assume that you have 1,000 PPC, which is 1% of the total PPC produced around the world. If your PPC reaches its maturation (meaning, it's ready to gain interest) and your share is still at 1,000 PPC, which is still 1% of the total PPCs, you will earn 10 PPC just for storing your coins in your wallet.

You need to unencrypt your wallet to start the minting process. Encrypted or locked wallets cannot be used for minting, so you need to remove your encryption for the time being. No need to worry as you will still need to input your passphrase for every transaction, so theft is not likely to happen during the process.

You will need to download, set up and configure the http://www.peercoin.net/downloads" software before you can start minting.

Your coins cannot be minted if they are not yet mature. The minimum coin age for minting is 30 days (after your last transaction) and the maximum is 90 days. Traded or transferred coins will be treated as fresh coins. This means that the age of the coin will be recounted, from the day it was received by its new owner. After 90 days, the coin cannot mature further and thus, cannot be used for minting.

Chapter 5:

Peercoin and The World

It was not long ago when a Star Trek Convention was held and Bitcoins were accepted in paying for entry passes and on-premise products.

Now that cryptocurrency is slowly gaining momentum in the world of commerce and trade, more and more merchants, whether online or not, are beginning to open their doors for cryptocoins such as Peercoin.

As of today, the following traders, business entities and charitable institutions are accepting Peercoin payments and donations:

SatoshiRoulette by SRoulette

Direct Voltage

Coin Gas Steam Codes

BTC Pipe Shop

Without Rule of Law

Bees Brothers

Jays Jerky and Goodies

All Things Luxury

Distinguished Imports

BitElectronics

Lucid Posters & Prints

CrownCloud

CINIPAC

CoinForWeb

Sierra Permaculture Design

Cryptocoin Send by Christian Eisenberg

Coin Payments

Sean's Outpost

Holy Angels Church

The Church of St. John the Evangelist

Voluntary Virtues

As of February of 2014, Peercoin is still working its way to worldwide acceptance. In addition, as the backbone of cryptocurrency, it is expected to gain more value as it gains more popularity.

Currently, 1 PPC is valued at $1.54 with a market cap of 32,810,782.00, and 21,303,857 PPCs are supplied, as of now.

Chapter 6:

The Future of Peercoin

There have been many questions as to how Peercoin can be a strong alternative to Bitcoin and how it can win against the competition.

On Being a Bitcoin Copycat

Peercoin was able to address issues and challenges created with Bitcoin, and this alone already says a lot about the currency. Peercoin is not a clone of Bitcoin. Yes, it follows the same ideology and yes, it uses similar protocols, but the whole system being used by Peercoin is certainly different from that of its counterpart.

Peercoin is an innovation, investing its interest in making a stable cryptocurrency without the fear of monopoly or 51% attacks. Its proof-of-stake scheme also proves to be a good feature since it is more energy-efficient and it creates an almost perfect inflation-free model. That same scheme also answers the issues of possible deflation.

On Having a Centralized Checkpoint

Enthusiasts of cryptocurrencies have always been cautious of supporting anything that is somewhat centralized. Peercoin started to operate with a central checkpoint to verify and validate each coin that goes out of its system. Since the idea behind cryptocurrency is decentralized distribution and security, the developer has somehow addressed this issue. In the latest version of the PPC software, central checkpoint became an optional feature for its users.

Regardless, the existence of central checkpoint was really temporary, just until the 51% attack was totally out of the question, then the checkpoint will be phased out completely. This just proves how Peercoin can adapt to the demands of its users and continue to grow as a technology, without giving up its best features.

On Ousting Bitcoin

Peercoin has never positioned itself to becoming the superior cryptocurrency. What peercoin is aiming for is to provide support, and thus co-exist with its fellow cryptocurrencies. So, the term "backbone" becomes a part of the argument. Peercoin is aiming for long-term value rather than become a day-to-day transactional tool.

On Proof-of-stake vs. Proof-of-work

These two systems work very differently. PoW will help miners get as many coins as they want, as long as they have the right resources to back it up. That opens a threat as it presents opportunities to monopolize the system.

The use of PoS will not cancel out the use of PoW. The proof of work will still be very useful in mining, and PoS will enhance it and make it a better system by getting rid of the possibilities of attacks.

On "Only the Rich get Richer"

Even in the traditional financial market, rewarding people for their investments and savings always makes a statement. These rewards are in the form of interests or rebates. The same principle applies to Peercoin minting. Would it be fair to dedicated miners if they stored their coins and mined for more and what they would receive is something less than those gained by people who never exerted any effort at all?

Two years is a pretty short time to judge a currency's future, especially its ability to establish itself amidst the competition. This does not seem to be the case with Peercoin, however. Peercoin has been mentioned in the likes of *The New York Times* and *Forbes* to be the most promising cryptocurrency and the best alternative to Bitcoin. Its fast growth and acceptance makes it a good addition to anyone's investment portfolio.

Conclusion

I hope this book was able to help you to learn about the basics of Peercoin, the different options you have, and how the future looks for this new currency. Now that you have learned the important factors about Peercoin, you can finally decide if you want to take the plunge, or if you can recommend it to your family and friends.

Plus, a little addition to your knowledge doesn't really hurt, right? It's good to know about new innovations because it keeps us in the know and up-to-date in a world where every big city has meet-up groups dedicated to learning more about cryptocurrencies.

Thanks again and good luck to you in your journey if you decide to get involved with cryptocurrency!

Conclusion